We dedicate this book to our son, Matthew Anderson.

He too appreciates a well managed restaurant.

Introduction

Restaurant management is both rewarding and complex. There are many rules, regulations and standards. It is built upon a large, diverse group of entry level employees, and has millions of customers to satisfy every day. This is a business that manufactures and sells its products within the same four walls every day. It takes special, detail oriented people, to make it all happen in a penny profit business. The pennies add up! Did you know the nation's 945,000 restaurants are projected to do about 580 billion dollars in sales in 2010?[1]

---

[1] National Restaurant Association, "Restaurant Industry Overview", 2010, <http://restaurant.org/research/facts/> (accessed March 1, 2010).

For us, it's about the people. We truly work with the best. Competitors and other businesses often attempt to recruit our managers. But they stay. They stay because we all genuinely care about one another. Like any business, there are good days and bad. But when you help one another grow and move forward each day as a team, relationships and bonds develop. This industry is filled with wonderful people and that is why we choose to work in restaurants.

We are a husband and wife team that has worked together in the restaurant industry for over 15 years. "He" is the QSR (quick service restaurant) Operator, and "She" is the Human Resources Director. Together, we have learned what it takes to be successful in restaurant management, and how to motivate, manage, and develop a very diverse group of people. These skills are applicable to any manager in any industry. We will share through "His" and "Her" perspectives and experiences.

From Her:

Scott grew up in a family of QSR operators that operated such brands as Wendy's, McDonald's, Taco Bell and Dairy Queen. Scott wanted to be a priest, but fortunately for me, he ultimately chose a career in the restaurant industry. Scott's first experience was at age 11, bussing tables. Scott accepted his first QSR job, as a manager trainee, in 1990. He graduated from Purdue University and then moved into human resources at a large QSR headquarters, before moving back into operations in 1995. That's when I entered the picture and we were married. Best decision that he ever made. He has since been a Director of Operations for several years. Together, we have over 43 years of restaurant experience. Wow that makes me feel old!

From Him:

Kelly grew up in Central Wisconsin and always wanted to marry someone just like me. Did I mention that she is older than I am? I also like to tease her about how she talks, "hey dere youz guyz." She may edit out my first three sentences. Kelly graduated from college with honors. She then worked for a large, upscale department store and was quickly moved into human resources because of her skills. She ultimately managed the HR (human resources) function for their largest store, which included three restaurants. Kelly was aggressively pursued by a large QSR brand and she too, in her designer dress and pumps, stereotyped our business and turned them down. Eventually she realized restaurant people are just like everyone else, and joined that large QSR. She has over 20 years of HR experience now under her belt. But she also has a passion and understanding of the entire QSR business, including operations. She can often be found in the restaurants in a skirt and heels, asking questions about QSC (quality, service and cleanliness) and profitability.

Table of Contents

Purpose

The purpose of writing this book is to share our thoughts, knowledge, experience and suggestions with anyone wanting to find success in restaurant management. We also hope to dispel some of the negative stereotypes associated with our business. We understand the stereotypes because we too were guilty of prejudging. We learned that restaurant people are the same professionals found in other industries. Now, in our current economy, which includes layoffs, downsizing, and overall instability, it is perfect timing to promote our business and the many opportunities within restaurant management. Luckily for us, people need to eat.

Honestly, we also hope the book pays for our son's dental work. Unfortunately for him, he is missing five adult teeth. Since we don't want to leave him toothless, we will be investing in several implants. Of course, Scott likes to remind me that it is hereditary and yes my family is the toothless bunch. Anyway, we hope the book helps you in some way, encourages you, reminds you where to focus your time, or that you at least enjoy the banter between me and Scott. Thank you.

QSC

Chapter 1

From Him:

The founding fathers of this industry liked to keep business simple and focused on standard procedures. To be a successful restaurant operator, you must remind yourself and your subordinate managers of that every day. Most of us lose sight of these basic operating procedures in this fast paced, ever changing environment. If you have ever worked in the QSR industry, there is no doubt that you have heard about QSC (quality, service and cleanliness). Those three letters guide us as we try to execute our jobs on a customer by customer basis. Focusing on QSC is how we keep it simple, basic and definitely how we find success. We have dedicated three chapters to quality, service and cleanliness. The QSC acronym is used so often that many front line operators forget the true meaning and value. Focus on QSC when training, coaching, setting goals and planning and the result will be a great customer experience and success for you.

It seems obvious, but evaluate QSC from the customer's perspective. We tend to put blinders on, even become complacent or numb to the things happening around us in the restaurant. Walk through your business as if you were a customer, this can help you see a situation more accurately, more objectively. Make the most of your time and always walk with a subordinate manager when possible. What is happening? Consistently evaluating your business with a critical eye and then making the necessary adjustments, is critical for a restaurant manager and for QSC. Some adjustments will need to be delegated to the appropriate employee, some adjustments may need to be written down for later follow-up, and there may be things you can take care of right then. Any time you can get something done immediately, just do it. For example, picking up two french fries that fell in the door way, pushing in a dining room chair, taking dirty trays to the back, or picking up a paper towel on the bathroom floor. As QSC is mentioned in this book, please pay close attention. In a restaurant focus on QSC, and you will be focusing on the basics. In this simplicity lies your success.

I like to think that no other industry enjoys the use of acronyms as much as ours. I have found that by adding the letter "P" to our favorite QSC acronym, that I am better able to remind myself and my team that this is a business. QSC&P (quality, service, cleanliness and profit), makes sense to me. When we mention success, success is profit. Without profit there is no business.

Cleanliness

Chapter 2

From Him:

You can't be a good restaurant operator and have a dirty restaurant. As a matter of fact, average cleanliness won't cut it either. I personally don't know anyone that was ever promoted above store level management that ran a dirty restaurant. A restaurant's cleanliness level is a direct indication as to how good of an operator you are. If your restaurant is dirty, you are not following the basics.

If your company doesn't provide you with cleaning systems, you're still accountable. In that case, create consistent systems to maintain equipment and overall cleanliness.

Now for the good news, taking a restaurant from a low or average level of cleanliness to an "A" level isn't that difficult. Kelly's advice will help.

From Her:

My wise, experienced uncle told me cleanliness comes first in this business. It comes before anything else. Think about it. Who wants to work in a dirty restaurant? Who wants to eat in a dirty restaurant? Who wants to risk making someone sick in a dirty restaurant? Even our son at age six, knew enough to check out the bathroom in a restaurant before ordering food. He wouldn't use the bathroom or eat there if it was dirty.

We stopped eating at one of our favorite pizza restaurants because it was dirty. The food was good but the cleanliness was terrible. They finally remodeled and made changes to their staff, but after eight years it was too late and customers had changed their eating patterns. Now they are clean but they struggle to stay in business.

If you don't know the difference between clean and dirty, don't bother to apply for a restaurant management position. The restaurant industry needs to have strict cleanliness and food safety guidelines, so we need to employ people that will enforce them.

There are health departments, county, state and federal laws that set some standards for cleanliness. Most companies also have specific standards and measuring tools. Just follow the rules. Make sure you and your people have the proper training offered and/or required. Use the proper tools in the proper manner. Procedures completed incorrectly, waste time and money because you won't get the desired results. Clean up your restaurant and maintain it. Be a role model and clean with your people. Train your people properly, explaining why. Delegate cleaning tasks daily and follow-up. Give feedback on how well the job was done. Do this every day, ask the same things, check the outcome, and give feedback. Never take for granted that a cleaning task will get done, or that it will be done properly. Most likely it won't. In fact expect that it won't. I should mention here, that restaurant management is full of repetition. You need to be comfortable asking the same things every day.

My uncle also told me, to assume is to blunder. I learned that concept quickly; when on the floor, on my belly pointing out dropped lids under an ice machine, I thought the manager took me seriously. Yet, the lids were still there the next day. I thought by pointing the lids out and asking that they be removed, that they would be. I was wrong, so now when I make a request, I personally follow-up and make sure it was done. Always follow-up. We have a chapter on follow–up because it is so critical to a manager's success. Also be specific when making a request. For example, ask, "When you get a break in service in the next half hour, clean under the ice machine please."

When training newer managers, I feel responsible for making cleanliness a priority in each of their minds. So, I tell a story about my son Matthew. Growing up with parents in the restaurant industry has made Matthew very aware of cleanliness and food safety. He makes sure his friends wash their hands after using the bathroom. He also frowns upon any type of double dipping when we entertain. While on vacation, we needed to use a restaurant restroom. Matthew, then age six, refused to use the bathroom after seeing a "turtle sundae" in the toilet bowl. A turtle sundae is made with chocolate and caramel. Get the picture? Our new managers do. They make faces and are disgusted. I want them to feel disgust and feel queasiness in their stomachs. I use examples so that cleanliness is always on the top of mind. I want managers to keep cleanliness a top priority and truly realize the impact it has on their business.

Our bottom line, keep your restaurant clean and safe.

Quality

Chapter 3

From Him:

My first job was in restaurant operations for a full
service restaurant, and I loved it. I had tried to stay away
from the negative stigma sometimes associated with the
quick service industry, even though that QSR business
had been very good to several of my family members. No
way was I going to be Flip-N-Burgers.

As a teen, I had an opportunity to visit the Pacific
Northwest for a week long spring break skiing trip.
Making an annual trip for snow skiing was always the

highlight of my year. My aunt and uncle asked that I spend the first day of my visit sitting in on a QSR manager orientation that was being conducted with a new hire. At the time I thought they wanted my feedback, I now realize that it was a typical Monday in the restaurant business and they were just too busy to go skiing. While sitting in on the orientation, I found myself intrigued by the quality. Fresh beef that is never frozen, served hot off the grill, just as it was ordered, with freshly prepared lettuce, onions and tomatoes, salads made fresh daily and homemade chili that took almost half a day to prepare and cook, all sounded surprising for a fast food restaurant. Back at the Haymarket (my first job), Roxy would always throw an extra order of catfish in the fryer just in case someone ordered it. Sometimes it was ordered, thirty minutes later. Looking back now, I can't believe they actually served that.

The trainee spent the day reading, watching training videos and listening to the Training Store Manager. The focus continued to be on quality. I was so impressed, that I called my aunt and asked if I could stay and work the lunch rush. I stayed with the trainee the entire week, had the time of my life, and never even made it to the mountain to ski. It was, in fact, quality that sold me on the QSR business.

Set procedures aid us in delivering a product the same way with the same great taste anywhere and at anytime. But what else does it take to make quality happen? It takes desire, consistency, pride and integrity. Quality begins with setting clear standards and expectations of your people, proper training, coaching, relentless follow-up and finally specific feedback. Much of the follow-up in a restaurant is quiet observation, focusing on one position at a time. Frequently, you have to watch the entire process of every task from beginning to end, in order to understand what your people are actually doing. Ensure your standards are being met and give feedback. Properly maintained equipment and strict food safety guidelines also impact quality. I believe the "fast" in fast food actually comes last on the priority list, with the first being cleanliness and the second being quality. Most customers would rather wait a little longer, than receive a substandard product quickly.

Training and
Development
Chapter 4

From Him:

One of my former bosses, Bob, asked me a
question a long time ago. He asked me what America's
favorite pass time was. Of course I answered the obvious,
baseball. He said no, it's going home and talking about
your job and your boss. He went on to point out that
because I was sitting in his office talking with him, my
employees were talking about me. In fact, when they

went home it would continue. I felt kind of sick as he continued. He told me it was my obligation to provide them the knowledge, tools and training to do their jobs successfully. Their livelihood depended on my ability to provide this.

Training is a part of and impacts several topics in this book, QSC&P, communication, follow-up, planning and waste. Training impacts adherence to policies and procedures, safety, productivity, efficiency and even employee morale. Therefore, training must be done properly and thoroughly. Most of us learn how important training is the hard way, after things go very wrong. By wrong I mean we experience customer complaints, a dirty restaurant, employee turnover, high food cost or high labor cost, just to name a few. If you have problems in your restaurant, re-evaluate your training practices first. You will need to plan time to train. We share planning tips later in the book.

If your company has a set training system, use it consistently. Remember different people learn differently, so be patient and ask lots of questions. Explain a task thoroughly, including safety tips and why it is done that way. Ask the trainee questions to ensure understanding. Watch the person perform the task and give specific feedback. If you delegate any part of training, make sure the trainer demonstrates the following:

- has good communication skills
- has patience
- is very knowledgeable of the task being trained
- has been taught how to effectively train
- trains by procedure, without shortcuts

Read our chapter on follow-up. You need to check what is actually happening, observe the training, ask the trainee questions, then watch the trainee perform the task. If you skip follow-up, I guarantee what you think is happening in your restaurant, isn't.

Cross training is valuable in the restaurants. The more tasks each person can do, the more flexibility you have as a manager. Managers always need two plans, plan A and plan B. Plan B is in case someone calls out sick, if business picks up or if business slows down. Plan B gives you flexibility. Plan B is something we usually use on a daily basis.

Training doesn't really end. Either we are learning something new or we are being re-trained. Don't forget that you and your managers need thorough training as well. I like to think that we are always trainees. One of our team's biggest mistakes is failing to continue training after a new manager has been placed. It is critical to his/her success that we stop in on shifts to see how things are going, to answer questions and to give feedback. Coaching and development must continue. This is the only way good habits can have time to form.

Coaching and giving specific feedback is how we keep employees doing the right things, the right way, as they were trained.

Development is continued training. A restaurant environment that includes development is an enjoyable place to work. People feel valued and see opportunity. Development is helping someone become stronger in their current position, or preparing them for another. Development requires goals, a written plan, and lots of feedback. You need to challenge and support the person. You delegate new tasks. This too will require training and feedback. Development is about caring enough to help another person. Development strengthens employees and the restaurant.

A development plan like the sample following, should be covered with the employee, agreed upon, and then followed up on. We suggest only two-three objectives at a time.

Sample Plan   Name: Bob, Assistant Manager

Development Objective	Action Plan	Follow-Up
1. To learn to write crew schedules.	-Meet with Mary for 2 hours of training before 11/5. -Write the 11/5 schedule with Mary. -Write the 11/12 schedule and have it reviewed by Mary before posting.	Weekly- Mary will review schedule and give feedback.
2. To give more on-line feedback.	-Give every employee two goals on every shift. -Give corrective and/or positive feedback throughout shift to every employee.	Daily- Mary observes and gives feedback to Bob.

In addition to developing new skills and improving weaker skills, we must also remember to leverage peoples' strengths. Utilize your people based on what they do well. It makes sense to put a friendly, outgoing employee on register. It makes sense for your organized subordinate manager to be in charge of filing. It makes sense for your fastest sandwich maker to make sandwiches through lunch.

A restaurant manager cannot run the business alone. We have to run our operation through other people. Training and development are critical factors in running good operations. Bob was right, training and development also set up employees for success. Success means an enjoyable environment to work in, plenty of hours available, and food on their families table. Training should be a priority for every manager.

Communication
Chapter 5

From Him:

As restaurant operators, we are communicating constantly, we are talking to customers, subordinate managers and entry level employees. Although I usually observe talk and some direction on my restaurant visits, often the communication is not specific or effective. Because goals and feedback are critical to QSC, I'd like to share what effective communication in this area looks like. Every employee should start their shift with at least one goal. When giving a goal, ask the employee to repeat or demonstrate what you have just asked of them. This helps ensure understanding. In my restaurants you will find each person has two goals. The first goal is related to some part of QSC, such as, proper hold times, thirty second service, saying thank you or wiping down your station during breaks in service. A QSC goal reminds everyone to impact the customer's experience. The second goal is related to profit, for example, proper portioning, suggestive selling or keeping food waste to a minimum. A profit goal helps people understand, every penny counts. This is a penny profit business, and when someone drops something on the floor, I take the opportunity to tell them specifically how much money they just lost. It's effective.

From Her:

I like to add something odd or unexpected when I'm speaking to our management group, because it helps keep everyone's attention and people tend to remember it. Recently we needed to encourage our managers to rethink their management style in this changing economy. I actually asked them to "lead like a lizard." We need to adapt to our environment, much like a chameleon does. As leaders, we need to make something happen by leading our people through it. We need to help them adapt along the way. We discussed in depth three skills that would help them, "lead like a lizard." We talked about coaching and development (see chapter 4), planning (see chapter 8) and communication.

Communication is important for so many reasons. How and what you communicate impacts employee morale, performance, productivity, turnover and profitability. Communication is key to influencing others and influencing others is key to leadership. As the leader, it is your responsibility to be an effective communicator. It is the only way the job will get done. I learned a valuable lesson in retail that applies to any service business. That is, "always be on stage." I don't mean be fake and insincere. I mean be nice, positive and smile, even if you don't feel like it. We owe that to our people and our customers. How can a rude, negative, sarcastic, crabby, manager ask his/her employees to be nice to customers? It doesn't make sense. Smile, be polite, be positive, and always expect the same of your team. If you have an employee on a headset working drive through, ask them to smile when speaking to the customer. It actually forces them to sound pleasant. If someone working register on the front line needs to smile and lighten up, ask them to lift their eye brows. I know this sounds odd but it works.

Listening is critical, so work at it. Don't be foolish and assume you are already a great listener. This is a skill that most of us work on for a lifetime. Sometimes I summarize or repeat key things, just to assure myself that

I'm listening and to reassure the person speaking with me. Listening makes people feel valued and respected. A good listener is always more effective. When you delegate a task, check for understanding. Ask specific questions. Listen to them as they repeat your request, because the employee may have misunderstood. Listening can eliminate misunderstandings and help ensure productivity. Also remember to make comfortable eye contact. Don't scare anyone by staring them down. And if you avoid eye contact, people may assume you are either weak or hiding something.

A manager should be confident, supportive and positive when communicating. Always explain "why" and be honest. I may not have the answer someone was hoping for, but I will explain and always be honest. People usually accept the situation and move on with their day because of the trust that has been built. Take ownership of what you are communicating. Stand tall and be self-assured. When you have to deliver a tough message or a message you might not agree with, don't say, "Mary said we have to do this." Take ownership of your message. Believe me your people will respect you more if the message comes from you. Your employees will be more likely to accept and move on. They count on you. If you find yourself passing the buck, talk to your supervisor and ask questions, adapt yourself before giving the message, get comfortable with it, then move forward.

Patience is so important, yet so difficult. Sometimes a situation or a person will drive you nuts. Take a deep breath, compose yourself and be patient. Things go wrong, people don't catch on as quickly as others and we are all very different, so accept that and relax. Maybe you need to rethink your own approach.

Finally, be flexible. Be flexible in how you think, in how you manage and in how you communicate. In a restaurant environment, with such a diverse group of employees, flexibility will help you adapt to both situations and people. Be open to questions and comments from your employees. Encourage two-way communication with your people. Create a restaurant with open communication where people feel comfortable working.

Communication abbreviated:

- Smile
- Be nice
- Be positive
- Show respect
- Take ownership
- Be flexible
- Be open minded
- Be professional
- Be pleasant
- Have patience
- Be honest
- Listen
- Be polite
- Explain why
- Be confident
- Give positive and corrective feedback
- Be supportive

- Make eye contact
- And don't forget to lift your eye brows if feeling tense or upset.

From Him:

There are ways to ensure communication happens in the fast paced, busy restaurants. We must give consistent feedback on line, both positive and corrective every day. The chapter on follow-up has some valuable tips. Coaching begins by giving goals and continues throughout the shift as you tell people how they are doing. Are they meeting the goals you gave them earlier? Specific feedback is accomplished by focused management, pausing to observe an employee's performance. Maybe you stop to watch a sandwich maker, watch them from the time they anticipate an order until the sandwich is complete and ready for the customer. What did the person do correctly, what do they need to do differently? Tell the employee and be specific.

It's helpful to give feedback at the end of a shift as well. Give a brief recap on how they did and thank them.

We suggest weekly meetings for the management team in a restaurant. A well planned, group meeting is an efficient way of sharing information. A manager should conduct planned one on one time with subordinate managers at least once per month. This is quiet, uninterrupted time to discuss performance and ask for their input. Hopefully your company has a formal performance evaluation process. This too will promote communication.

Recognize good performance in front of others and consider having a formal recognition program. A simple thank you also goes a long way. We often remind ourselves and our managers to catch people doing something right. This reinforces good behaviors. Positive communication helps create a positive restaurant environment.

Follow-up

Chapter 6

From Him:

Looking back, I learned a lot from my first store manager. Sometimes we learn more from people's mistakes. He was well liked and could work any position in the restaurant better than his employees. We know a great sandwich maker does not necessarily make a great manager. The other restaurants in the same company were making much larger profits. We did nothing in our store to drive profit. We didn't discuss issues like waste, over portioning, over ordering, theft or accurate inventories. He didn't even worry about the number of employees on the floor (labor cost), unless his boss was there. I remember thinking this is supposed to be a million dollar business and we are taking our profit right out to the parking lot and burning it. My uncle says that and it paints an accurate picture. My father was a banker and if I wanted to just watch a million dollars be exchanged I could have gone to the bank. I didn't want to look at someone else's money and I certainly didn't want to burn it. I wanted to learn how to make money.

My manager lost money because he took the basic standards of the business for granted. He expected that the right things would just happen, so he never bothered to enforce them. Standards are everywhere in our industry. Our operations manual is full of them. We have policy manuals, training materials plus county, state, and federal standards. We have so many standards that we sometimes take for granted that they are being met every day. My first manager made this mistake, among others. It was clear to me even then, you need to have standards, including personal standards and enforce them every day with every employee. If you do there will be profit. But how do you enforce standards? You do this through role modeling, training, feedback and follow-up. Most of us have learned the hard way, that follow-up is usually the step that gets missed.

From Her:

You have to plan in order for follow-up to happen consistently. Specific follow-up needs to be part of a written plan. You will read more about planning in an upcoming chapter. If you set a standard, you must check that it has been met. Assume that it won't be and always check. Follow-up needs to become habit and part of what you do every day. Watch what your people are doing and stop, observe and ask questions. Most of us make the mistake of assuming a standard was met, of course we were wrong, and now we will likely face consequences. The result could be a dirty restaurant, a food safety issue, waste, a customer complaint, theft or turnover, just to name a few.

I often hear managers frustrated because something didn't get done right or didn't get done at all. Follow-up with specific feedback is the answer to their problem. When you check something that was done properly, thank the person. Give recognition for even small successes. If it wasn't done right, give specific, corrective feedback. I like to have the person redo it. Then I return to give positive reinforcement. After a correction, I always advise that you return and "catch" the person doing it right.

Never underestimate the impact of follow-up. A manager that consistently follows up is very likely to be successful in restaurant management. We try to make this point to our own management group again and again. Follow-up is an effective use of a manager's valuable time. It must be a big part of his/her written weekly plan.

Goals

Chapter 7

From Him:

If you're anything like me, working goals, planning and being organized are things that don't come naturally. In fact, I have always thought that I was pretty good in this area, until Kelly told me otherwise. I believe that because taking care of the customer is so much easier than taking care of the business, we spend more of our time serving the customer. Actually running the business is taking care of our customer. We will execute (QSC) better, more consistently, longer term.

51

Many managers in our industry have moved into management internally from front line service roles. We might be good at setting positional type goals, or planning for that lunch rush, or even organizing the walk-in refrigerator before a large delivery. That is not enough. Don't fool yourself into thinking that you can skip over these next two chapters because they don't apply to you. For years, I thought they didn't apply to me.

When Kelly presented this material to my entire management and multi-unit team and held us accountable for following through, we began making the biggest strides in my entire career. I owe her for pushing us so hard. I spent many years tending to on-line service and the employees' daily needs while neglecting the fact that we were running a business. As a manager you put the customer first by running your business.

From Her:

Goals, planning and organization really do go hand in hand. No manager or leader can truly be successful without this. Let's begin with goals. Why have goals you ask? It is the leader's responsibility to the team to set goals, that if achieved, bring about success. It's your job. If no one knows what to focus on and everyone is doing their own thing, what do you end up with? Yes, chaos, confusion, a dirty restaurant, inconsistency and so on. This is not success. Employees won't want to work there for long, overall productivity will be low, waste will be high and profit won't exist.

So let's begin with goal setting. There are many books on this topic in great detail so I just want to keep it simple. It's great for multi-unit managers to have yearly and quarterly goals. These goals should impact the monthly/weekly goals for the restaurants. I find that managers with monthly goals reflected in weekly plans, tend to be more successful, as they are simple, broken down into bite-size pieces, top of mind and happening now. Therefore, I will focus on monthly goals in this chapter. How does a manager come up with a goal? In the restaurants there are so many things to work on, always a list of things to get done, unexpected challenges that pop up, employee issues and something due to your boss before you leave for the day. How do you decide?

First, ask yourself what isn't going well in your restaurant. Goals are intended to move you forward, fix, strengthen or better a situation. You could ask your boss, since I'm sure he/she will have some suggestions. As I stated earlier, your issues are probably part of their goals already. Have paper in hand and make a list. If you or your company conducts evaluations on the restaurant, those evaluations will have specific areas of opportunity. They are valuable tools. You can also meet with your management team to brainstorm and agree on things that need to be addressed. Group discussions are an effective way to get the necessary buy-in to actually make change and meet the goals set.

Now you have a list. You can't take on too many things at once, or nothing will get done. Analyze your list. Does anything stand out, is there an obvious priority? Maybe one thing on the list impacts several others. Maybe there is something that impacts food safety. Rank your list by priority, starting with #1. Now you will be clear on what two or three things should be your priorities. Hang on to your list, as you will use it in the next chapter. You will use your monthly goals to create weekly plans.

Planning and Organization

Chapter 8

From Him:

This chapter talks about many of the weaknesses that I struggled with early in my career. In fact, "She" would tell you that I still struggle in this area. Ah, the joy of working with your wife.

I have found that many people struggle here because they don't realize this is part of the foundation needed to be successful. So read carefully.

From Her:

Planning is one of my favorite things to do. People that know me accuse me of being a bit obsessive, compulsive, tightly wound and even anal. I think it's a good thing to have your holiday cards and shopping done by October. The boxes are all wrapped and ready to go. I like to think I'm just special.

Managers plan for success. Weekly plans need to be written. If you have a computerized program, that's fine. I prefer a 6 3/4" by 8 1/2" spiral bound weekly planner. It shows me a week at a glance and includes dates and time. Some managers use a single sheet of paper to write their plan. It should be labeled for each day of the week and have ample space to make a list under each day. Your company likely has a form, but you could also check the internet or an office supply store.

Please return to the sheet of paper that has your goals written on it. Turn it over and write down the two or three goals you determined were your priorities. Take one goal at a time and think about what you have to do to make it happen. What action steps must be done in order to achieve that goal? Be very specific. Write these action steps under the goal. Break it down into the "how". Think about who will need to do each action step. Will they need training? Will they need follow-up? When will this need to happen? How will it be communicated? Actually as a manager, follow-up will be much of what you write on your plan. The more specific you can be, the better your weekly plan will be.

Example: Goal- to make sure morning checklists are being done. (This goal was chosen because it will impact the restaurant's food cost, morning labor waste and cleanliness issues).

The action steps necessary might include discussion at a managers' meeting. Subordinate managers need to understand what is expected, know how to complete the task effectively, understand their role and know why it is important. A managers' meeting is an effective, efficient way to communicate this. Another action step might be training. If one of the subordinate managers is new to the team, he/she needs to see how this task is completed. How can he/she do a task correctly if he/she doesn't know what a good job looks like? Specifically, the action step could be training time with you. This might include time set aside in the dining room explaining the task verbally, time on a specific day where he/she watches you perform the task or another day when you observe him/her complete the task and give feedback. Another action step could be follow-up. You will need to personally check if the morning checklists are being done and if they were completed to the standards you set. I know this sounds tedious and insanely detailed. But that's our business, full of the same details every day. Once you get comfortable with it, an organized, detail oriented, well planned leader manages this business with ease.

Sample Plan:

Goal: To make sure morning checklists are being completed.

	Monday	Tuesday	Wednesday	Thursday
8am				
9am	food order	train Mary checklists – I do it...	observe Mary do checklist	check morning checklist
3pm	managers' meeting – discuss checklists			
4pm				
5pm			crew schedule	
6pm	one on one w/Mary checklists			
7pm		Mom's Birthday		

Now we write your weekly plan. Using your planner of choice, the computer, a spiral planner like mine, or a single sheet of paper, first fill in your schedule for the week. I suggest plotting the "givens" next. A given is something routine that must be completed, for example a Monday morning food order, a Wednesday afternoon managers' meeting, writing schedules, etc. I also suggest noting personal givens, such as a dentist appointment, mother's birthday, soccer practice, etc. Now review your 2-3 goals and action steps. Action steps should now be written on your plan. Only you will know what makes sense to do each day, based on your schedule, other commitments, business flow, etc. Again much of what you write will probably be some type of follow-up. Fill them in, be realistic and don't over commit. I suggest using a timeline each day, listing morning tasks first, then late morning, afternoon, and finally evening. If your planner doesn't include specific time, for example 8a.m.,

9a.m., 10a.m., etc., I suggest filling specific time in. That will help you know what you need to do, or where you need to be with a quick glance. Any time saving tips are important in our business.

Here are three more tips. Post this where you and your subordinate managers can see it. Out of sight really does mean out of mind. Other managers will appreciate being included, learn about planning and be more likely to help. And as things come up during the week that you need to do or remember, add them to your plan. A manager that writes things in several places, has lots of notes on various pieces of paper, or tries to trust everything to memory, is not productive or efficient. Many managers have told me that they get more accomplished with a written plan. They also accomplish more of the critical things that impact their goals, and make progress. Progress feels good. Finally, set aside time each week to write your plan for the following week.

Yes, plan to plan. I believe anything that is planned for in a restaurant, is more likely to go well.

Organization is not a trait that everyone shares. Not all managers are organized, but a leader recognizes his/her shortcomings and compensates. If you are not organized, either learn how to be or hire an organized subordinate manager. Our business is too complex not to have organization. Disorganization results in turnover, theft, waste, policy/procedure violations, cleanliness issues, loss of productivity, chaos, confusion and stress. The back room, office, drawers, shelves, cupboards, outside storage and walk-ins need to be kept organized every day. I love to remind managers, a place for everything and everything in its place. An organized restaurant creates efficiency and a stable environment for your employees.

Waste Not

Chapter 9

From Him:

Controlling waste, if done correctly can lead to a very successful career in the restaurant industry. However, before you can control waste, you really need to understand what waste is. As odd as it may sound, most managers really don't understand that waste control goes beyond controlling food.

As newcomers to the restaurant industry we learn rather quickly that wasting food is not a good thing. The QSR industry in particular, is inundated with procedures to help control food waste. For example, scraping every last drop of mayonnaise out of the container it came in and applying just the right amount on each bun, prevents us from giving away profit. Why overstuff a fry carton, only to drop several on the floor? Every position in a restaurant has an opportunity to help control waste and this must be communicated to each employee through training, coaching and follow-up. As managers we need to look for the right or wrong behaviors and give feedback.

Most managers are naturals at understanding how important controlling food waste is. They watch many areas like, proper portioning, hold times, order accuracy and not over prepping. Two more areas that require a manager's attention are theft and proper ordering.

For a new manager, responsibility for the profit and loss statement can be overwhelming. They usually understand the importance of controlling product waste.

The new and more challenging areas are labor, paper and utilities. They must learn quickly that these potential areas of waste must also be controlled in order to be successful.

Labor is expensive, so you should only have the minimum staffing required, based on business at any given time. Schedule appropriately and send people home if need be. Many companies look at sales per man hour to help gauge proper staffing. People must be productive. Training, goals, coaching and follow-up are critical to maximizing productivity.

Paper cost is also important to be aware of. Paper goods should be only ordered when necessary. To keep shelves full of goods you don't need, costs money. This inventory on your shelves is money you have not even earned yet. Teach employees not to be careless by dropping items on the floor, which is very costly. Much of utility cost is a given, but if you stage equipment turn on you can save dollars. Some equipment can be turned on just before open. The store thermostat that regulates your heating and cooling system can be monitored and set economically. Equipment that is properly maintained also saves money.

We should always be learning from those around us and never miss an opportunity to benefit from someone else's experience. After all, this is a penny profit business and managing it well takes skill and effort. This year Walt, our uncle, challenged our management team to a war on waste. Waste was described as anything that we as managers could control. This included food, paper, labor, productivity and even our own time. He challenged us to spend "our" time getting results through training, coaching and performance management. He has always told us if we take care of the business, then it will take care of us.

Most of us have learned the hard way, if you're not detailed in monitoring waste, profit slips through your fingers quickly. Waste management will be worth your effort.

Our tips for waste management:

- As a manager, write the schedules yourself. This has a considerable impact on labor. Be flexible and always be open to more efficient ways to schedule. Schedule around business needs, not just to give someone hours. Why schedule two managers at the same time if you could schedule one manager and an entry level employee? Why have too many people on the floor when business is slow?

- Send employees home early if business is slower than expected. Make sure your subordinate managers do the same. This has been an area of labor waste for us. People must react quickly. You must personally check to make sure this is happening.

- Control overtime. Why pay 1.5 or 2 times the cost of labor?

- As the manager, do the ordering yourself. Over ordering results in costly waste. If you over order food, it may go bad. Over ordered food and paper is also excess stock that must be paid for early. Why pay for something now that you won't use for 1-2 weeks?

- Check in incoming orders yourself. Make sure you are receiving what is listed on the invoice and that the quality is acceptable. This prevents theft, being shorted and substandard quality.

- Make thorough training a priority. Train proper procedures, portioning, and train people to be productive. This is so critical, there is more to it than you may realize. Read the chapters on training and follow-up. Without follow-up effective training won't happen. You need to check what people are doing and make sure things are being done to your standards. Inspect what you expect. If you train someone to fill ice to the fill line, watch them do it. And watch them do it again. Training and follow-up will make a big impact on waste.

- When assigning tasks give time goals.

- Make sure morning prep is being done correctly. Over prepping, results in throwing out food. Waste can also occur if prep procedures are not being followed. If lettuce is being cut wrong, the employee might be throwing out usable product. Set standards for your morning prep team, train them well and check in on them often.

- Watch for theft. This too really impacts waste. Anyone could be a thief. I don't mean treat people badly, I mean be cautious and never take anything for granted. Always enforce all policies. Everyone on your team should know that theft is unacceptable. Employees will come to you if they know someone is stealing, as long as they trust it will be handled appropriately. Never tolerate theft of any kind. People steal money out of their register, by pocketing cash, by ringing in fraudulent transactions, or by deleting transactions just to name a few. People steal uncooked product like sleeves of meat. Employees have extra condiments like cheese added to their sandwich without paying for it. This too is theft. People take box cutters, supplies, knives, straws, jars of pickles, brooms, window cleaner, and yes, even toilet paper. People steal time by falsifying their time cards. Really almost anything can and will be stolen. I should add that some people eat product right on line. Popping a french fry into your mouth on line is theft. You have to always be aware and be looking for theft. Sometimes it's the person you least expect, but believe me theft happens all the time. Adhering to policies and frequent inventories can be helpful in preventing theft.

- I've mentioned giving each employee a profit goal on every shift. I went into this in more detail in another chapter. But remember, whatever is important to you, will become important to your team. The goals you give and the coaching that follows will make profitability a priority for your employees.

- Make sure all employees know that pay increases, bonuses and hours are only possible if there is profit. Waste eliminates profit, so make waste personal to your team by explaining it.

- A manager should always clock employees in and out.

- Keep the office and storage areas locked. Limit keys.

- Always follow and enforce all policies.

- Food leftovers and mistakes should be thrown out and considered waste. Never allow this food to be eaten. This only encourages more mistakes.

- Monitor proper portioning and order accuracy carefully. Both are costly mistakes that add up quickly.

- Don't allow employees to determine amounts of prep. Employees should know to come to you for how much lettuce to cut or how many chicken breasts to cook.

- Keep employees busy at all times. Goals and coaching help to ensure people are doing the right things.

- Turnover is very costly. Make sure to create an environment that encourages people to stay. Happy, trained employees tend to stick around.

- As a manager, always have a weekly plan. This ensures you will be working on the right things. Your time is very valuable, don't waste it.

Bottom line, if you waste in the restaurants, you won't be in business for long.

Human Resources

Chapter 10

From Him:

Not all operators make good HR people. I didn't, in Kelly's opinion. I got tired of listening to people whine and couldn't wait to get back into the restaurants. But human resources and the people that do it well really lend critical support to our business. They make sure we follow policies and that we are consistent in our practices. They balance us and yes, keep us out of litigation. At the risk of inflating her ego, I appreciate what "She" does for us.

From Her:

Wow, thanks for the boost Scott! It is my pleasure to discuss my favorite topic, HR.

As a manager, you are ultimately responsible for the environment of your restaurant. I wanted our managers to understand their role and take ownership. So I did an exercise at a monthly meeting. I passed a mirror around and had each person look into it and say out loud, "I am the leader. It's all up to me". After passing the mirror, I explained that if the restaurant is running poorly, it is "your" fault. And if all is running well, that too is "your" fault. If you truly buy into that, you have taken a big step toward success. If you take personal responsibility, you will search internally for causes of restaurant issues. And then you will work to resolve them. Unfortunately many managers spend their time pointing fingers, blaming others and wait for someone else to fix their problems. That never works long term. Again, you are ultimately responsible for the environment of your restaurant. Look in the mirror.

HR, is in fact, all about creating a stable, safe, fair, and professional environment, where people feel comfortable working.

The following is a list of helpful HR suggestions from me to you:

- Be someone you would want to work for.
- Be a role model for all that you ask or expect.
- Be consistent, fair and always error on the side of the employee.
- Follow all policies and procedures and expect the same of your people.

- Make new hire orientations a priority. Be thorough, don't delegate this task.
- Give consistent feedback. Be honest and specific.
- Address the behavior, not the person.
- Create open two-way communication in your restaurant.
- Treat everyone with respect. Yes everyone.
- Be pleasant, positive, friendly, polite and professional everyday, no matter what.
- Smile even if you don't particularly feel like it.
- Listen, listen, listen...

The following have proven successful for us over the years:

- Never mess with anyone's pay. Enforce and comply with all federal and state employment standards. I tell our managers, when in doubt, pay it out.

- All required meal and rest periods must be given, no excuses.

- Schedule fairly. Give hours based on performance, not based on who you like.

- If you cut hours based on performance, discuss with the employee before doing so.

- Don't suspend for punishment. I only suspend pending a serious investigation where the likely outcome is termination.

- Be consistent in interviewing practices and always use a two interview process.

- Hold weekly meetings with your management team. Once per month, hold one on ones with each subordinate manager.

- Don't allow fraternization. Hopefully your company has a written policy regarding this.

- Don't tolerate theft, violence, drugs, threats, harassment of any type, or anything else that could threaten someone's safety or your restaurant's environment. Hopefully your company has written policies to support you.

- Always make employee safety/security a top priority. Enforce your policies.

- Be consistent in your practices, and when issuing written warnings or terminating employment.

- Document employee issues such as performance discussions, attendance, warnings, investigations, etc. Be specific, who, what, where, when, any witnesses. Only document facts not your opinion.

Good documentation helps ensure fairness, consistency and memory. Yes memory. For example, if you receive an unemployment claim from a year ago, will you remember details? Not likely. Notes will help you recall the facts and better defend your position. I have included a sample warning form in case you don't have one. This form has worked well for us. I ask our managers to keep written warnings simple and specific. Details, like where, when, or witnesses, can be written on a separate piece of paper for future reference.

Sample Warning:

WARNING

Date: _____ Employee Name: _____

This is a warning for:

	Absence		Rude to employee or customer
	Tardiness		Failure to follow instructions
	Cash control violation		Violation of safety procedures
	Unsatisfactory work quality		Insubordination
	Using abusive or inappropriate language		Abuse of equipment/property
	Violation of company policy/procedure		Other

Manager's
Explanation_____
_____
_____
_____
_____

Further incidence of a similar nature, may result in further disciplinary action up to and including termination.

Employee: _____ Manager: _____

Harassment is a topic all managers should be trained on. If your company doesn't offer specific training, consider looking for something offered in your community. This would be time well spent. Much of HR is simply preventing issues like harassment. The more you know, the better you can handle situations effectively and hopefully prevent them all together. I am not an attorney and this is certainly not a book about harassment, but I will give you a few things to consider:

- Don't tolerate harassment of any kind.

- Know the laws and your company policy, and know what not to tolerate.

- Things like jokes, swearing, sexual talk, sexual gestures, any kind of touching, sarcasm, anger, put downs, name calling and yelling, should not be allowed.

- Keep the restaurant environment professional.

- Make sure employees know who they can go to with concerns.

- Make sure subordinate managers are trained on what to do in a situation or if someone comes to them with a complaint.

- Customers or vendors can also harass. Know what to do in these situations.

- Appropriately address small employee issues/concerns promptly and you will likely avoid bigger problems like harassment.

- Be a professional role model.

- Create an environment with open communication, where people feel comfortable coming to you. This is a great prevention tool.

- Know how to conduct a proper investigation. This will help you resolve harassment issues as well as other serious issues that may come up. Get training.

These are some of the guidelines we follow when conducting an investigation:

- Be prompt, within 24 hours if possible.

- Take notes yourself. Don't take written statements.

- Don't delegate any part of the investigation.

- Prepare your questions in advance.

- Ask specifics, such as who, what, when, why, where, how, any witnesses, any prior incidents, have you told anyone, anything else I need to know.

- Ask each person for their confidentiality.

- Conduct only one on one interviews, not group interviews.

- Interview the complaining employee first.

- Interview witnesses after the complaining employee.

- The last interview is conducted with the person the complaint was against.

- Don't make personal judgments or comments, just get the facts.

- Don't share anything with others on your team, including managers. Only inform people that need to know, like your supervisor or human resources professional.

- After appropriate action is determined and complete, meet again with the complaining employee. This is important so the person knows you handled the situation. I always take the opportunity to remind the employee to come forward anytime he/she has concerns.

I need to end this chapter with a disclaimer. My experience is in human resources, not employment law. I can only share what has worked for us. Please consult an attorney for any legal advice. Remember, as a manager, the work environment is in your hands. You need to be doing the right thing at all times.

Happy People

Chapter 11

From Her:

During a monthly meeting, I asked our managers to treat our people like gold. I handed each manager a small gold fabric pouch tied with a piece of gold ribbon. They were each asked to open one. Inside they found several gold nuggets, small painted stones. Each nugget represented one of their subordinate managers. I went on to explain how their people were very valuable, just like gold. I reminded them of all the time and effort that went into recruiting, training, coaching, and managing each person. I asked the managers to think about all the tasks these employees did for them. I talked about how difficult and costly it would be to replace their teams. Employees are truly as precious as gold and should be treated as such.

We count on our teams every day to take care of our customers. So we must take good care of them. Always be good to your people. This sounds so simple, yet so many managers don't treat their people right. We can't afford to take them for granted.

From Him:

I...

Back to Her:

You what? I need to step in and write this chapter. Sorry Scott.

On occasion, Scott himself walks around with a crabby scowl. I have to ask him to look in a mirror or to lift his eye brows in hopes of improving his facial expression. From time to time, I request that he take a deep breath and loosen up. As managers we need to be "happy" role models every day, on every shift, no matter what. This is an essential part of our job.

Any restaurant manager will tell you that consistent staffing plays a big role in their success and their sanity. Keeping employees happy is not an easy task, yet it is critical to minimizing turnover. Turnover is costly for restaurants due to time spent training, lower productivity, waste from mistakes and slower service just to name a few. So how do you keep a diverse group of people happy in a hectic, fast paced restaurant environment? You do this with thorough training, effective communication and consistent practices in human resources. Three chapters have been dedicated to these topics, because of the impact on employee morale and the work environment.

Training, if done right gives people a sense of accomplishment and pride. Based on your communication skills, people may be motivated to work hard for you. On the other hand, if your skills are lacking, employees may become slackers, or may not even show up. Communication is very impactful in restaurants. It would be worthwhile to re-read the "Communication Abbreviated" list. The function of human resources is to create a stable, safe, professional environment where people feel comfortable working. When employees feel comfortable, confidence is high.

Schedules are also very important to your employees. This is often emotional for people because it directly impacts their personal life. When writing a schedule you must accomplish two things. You need to meet the business needs and be flexible and understanding of employees' needs at the same time. If this sounds ridiculous to you, you will likely not retain your people.

Here are some tips to consider:

- Know what matters most to each of your people and make it important to you. If Sally has baseball every Wednesday night, give her that night off. If Mark only sees his son on Monday's, don't schedule him that day.

- Post the schedule at minimum, one week in advance, and don't be late.

- Make sure your people know how to make schedule requests and honor them whenever possible.

- I suggest writing monthly schedules for managers.

- Meeting as a management team to complete manager's schedules can be very effective. Everyone in the group will be more willing to share in what must be done. Give and take helps people be accepting because they perceive fairness.

- A group meeting is a great way to plan vacations for the year.

We also have to treat people with respect and talk nicely to them at all times. Remember when I said to smile even if you don't feel like it, this is the same thing. Be positive and upbeat even if you are having a bad day. Maybe three people didn't show up for their shift, or you argued with your spouse before work. It doesn't matter, put a smile on and adjust your attitude accordingly. Employees will perform for a manager that treats them nicely, politely and respectfully. Say thank you often. If you can't be pleasant, work in a non-service industry, because no one will want to be around you, much less work for you. I'm not saying be insincere or overlook poor performance.

Address unacceptable behavior calmly and professionally, don't make it personal or show any anger. We all get angry. Take a deep breath, cool off and plan your performance conversation. Address the situation in private when you are composed. Explain what behavior needs to be changed, be clear on what you expect, discuss consequences and ask for any questions. Teams appreciate a manager that holds people accountable to policies and procedures. Most of us prefer working in a clean, orderly, organized, friendly work environment.

Now this brings up another point. Don't overdo the friendliness. You can't be a buddy, or hang out after work with your people. There is a fine line and you must find it. Most managers end up learning from mistakes here. Just trust me and don't have any personal relationships outside the restaurant with your employees. What? You don't believe me? Let me share some examples. Employees won't take you seriously at work or listen to you after watching what you did playing truth or dare the night before. One of your work pals said you did something inappropriate outside of work with another employee and now there is a lawsuit against the company and you. Employees don't want to work with you because they perceive favoritism and now they are complaining to your supervisor. Get the picture- the manager never wins. Be pleasant to everyone without being their buddy.

Finally, you need to make sure your subordinate managers are creating the same environment on their shifts. They need to treat people with respect. But how do you enforce it? First you need to role model proper behavior at all times, no excuses. You need to set clear, specific expectations of them, and then you need to follow-up on their shifts. Make surprise visits often on your managers' shifts, then look and listen to what is going on.

For example:

- Is the store clean and the team organized?

- Listen to Mary working drive-through register. Is she using a proper greeting, is she upbeat, is she thanking customers?

- Is the manager coaching employees with a smile and good attitude?

Also ask employees specific questions. You could ask each person what their goals are. Ask how the shift is going. Finally, give your manager specific feedback and explain the expectations again if necessary. Be specific and thank them for what they did well.

In summary, you will create happy people by creating a good work environment. Keep the restaurant clean and organized. Provide thorough training. Ensure professional communication. Be consistent and fair. Remember to be flexible in scheduling. And make sure everyone on the management team is upbeat, pleasant and R.E.S.P.E.C.T.F.U.L.

Happy employees create satisfied customers, which in turn makes for a very successful manager.

Back to Him:

I had to sneak this in after the final edit of the book. You guessed it, Kelly is the happy one, and I'm sometimes accused of being crabby. Focus, passion and the desire to be the best can sometimes show on my face. But "She" is right. The restaurant environment is critical and it is your responsibility. We are fortunate to have managers and a multi-unit team that work hard to maintain a good environment for our people. You will need to do the same in your restaurant.

Service

Chapter 12

From Her:

Imagine you're in a quick service restaurant waiting in a very slow line. It's finally your turn to order. The register operator could not care less and doesn't even make eye contact. She pushes your change towards you and starts talking to the next customer. A tray with food is pushed your way and no one says a word to you. Now you sit down at a dirty table, open your sandwich only to find mayonnaise...You told the register operator no mayo. Now you get up and try to weave through people to get back to the counter. No one looks your way, you seem to be invisible. So you speak out and say, "Excuse me my sandwich is wrong." A girl grabs the sandwich and rolls her eyes. She tells you this is the way you ordered it. You try to explain, but the register operator jumps in and tells you that's how you ordered it. Let's stop here, because typing this is irritating me. The customer experienced order inaccuracy, indifference, arguing, rude behavior, a dirty restaurant, slow service and not even a thank you. Why would a customer want to put themselves through this? They wouldn't and they won't be back. If you tolerate this type of behavior, you won't be in business for long.

Service attitude is something we must role model at all times. At our monthly managers' meeting I wanted our team to understand the impact of role modeling. So I started the meeting with fun dancing music and actually danced myself. There were some snickers and some people seemed uncomfortable. I just laughed and continued to dance around the conference room with each individual. There were smiles and most managers joined in and danced with me. We all had a laugh and enjoyed the few minutes of spontaneity. Then I made my point. As managers we have so much influence over our employees' behavior, just by what we do. As I danced and laughed, others did too. If we role model happy, courteous, friendly service, our employees will be more inclined do the same.

I'd like to be clear, if you don't truly enjoy "serving" others, don't work in a service industry. It is a big part of what we do. The only reason we are in business, is because of our loyal customers. Giving excellent service is the way to keep them. I ask our managers to be noticeably nice. We need to smile, be pleasant, polite, helpful and very, very appreciative. We need to expect the same of all our employees. Challenge your team to remember customers' names. And if we make a mistake, apologize, fix it and apologize again. Never give excuses or argue. Our customers are invaluable, they basically sign our paychecks. Why then is this the shortest chapter and why have we put it at the end of our book? Because each previous topic and chapter, create the customer service needed to be successful.

We would like to sincerely thank all of our customers for their patronage, and for continuing to eat out on occasion. Everything we do as operators is about you and for you. Without you, "we" would not be.

Career Opportunities

Chapter 13

From Him:

Flip-N-Burgers is big business and don't let anyone fool you into thinking that it's a dead end job for people that can't do anything else. During my career, people have negatively stereotyped me and the people I work with because of what we choose to do for a living. I've seen and heard just about everything. I've had sandwiches thrown at me, and been called names. One of my coworkers likes to remind me of the time a customer asked him, who that beady-eyed bozo standing over there was. Yes it was me. I wish I had a dollar for every time someone looked at me in disbelief when I told them where I work. I love to tell people that I flip burgers and usually prefer working fries. I am truly proud to be in the burger business.

Dave Thomas, the founder of Wendy's was so proud of his business, that in the early days all company employees had to wear the same uniform that was worn in the restaurants. It didn't matter if you were in restaurant operations or in any of the support departments like marketing or legal. Everyone wore the white and blue stripes and the hat. Now that's being proud.

From Her:

I understand the stereotypes, because I too was guilty of prejudging the restaurant industry. I quickly learned that restaurant people are the same professionals that you find in other industries. We look like other people. We don't have horns. I am proud to tell people where I work. I do think it surprises them and actually helps dispel the negative stereotypes. People still ask, "hamburgers?" As if they heard me wrong. I always repeat, yes burgers. Then the person looks me up and down, maybe looking for the horns. People also expect me to be over weight. I tell them I'm not because we offer quality food and healthy menu options. Yes, I eat it every day.

I have to tell one story because it will be forever etched in my memory. While at a full-service restaurant, dining with very close friends, they told us about their son getting his first job. They were so thrilled he didn't have to work fast food. We almost choked on our dinner. I politely offered a job with us if something fell through. I really wanted to pull the bottle of wine out of his hands that we undesirables had just paid for. I must add that the restaurant industry has been very good to us. We enjoy what we do and it has afforded us a nice life style.

Back to Him:

As I shared earlier, the nation's 945,000 restaurants are projected to do 580 billion dollars in sales in 2010.[2] Wow, who wouldn't want a piece of that? Many restaurant managers are responsible for well over one million dollars in sales a year, even at fast food restaurants with average checks of five dollars. I know there are people working in management, in other

---

[2]National Restaurant Association, "Restaurant Industry Overview", 2010, <http://restaurant.org/research/facts/> (accessed March 1, 2010).

industries, that look down on what I do. But truth be known, many aren't responsible for anything close to a million dollars. And I doubt most possess the high level of management skills that we look for when hiring a store manager.

The United States Department of Labor, Bureau of Labor Statistics, expects job openings to be abundant in our industry. They anticipate excellent opportunities for jobseekers through the next decade. Nearly 1 in every 10 American workers is working in a food and beverage related industry.[3] The National Restaurant Association reports that nearly half of all adults have worked in the restaurant industry at some point, and that more than 1 in 4 adults got their first job experience in a restaurant.[4] No other industry has touched so many people's lives. Couple

---

[3] Bureau of Labor Statistics, "Career Guide to Industries, 2010-11 Edition", 2010-11, < http://www.bls.gov/oco/cg/cgs023.htm> (accessed March 2, 2010).
[4] National Restaurant Association, "Jobs and Careers", 2009, < http://www.restaurant.org/careers/> <accessed May 11, 2009).

that with the fact, that on a typical day, more than 130 million individuals will be foodservice patrons and then tell me that this isn't big business. Industry statistics like these create significant career opportunities for those of us already in the industry, and for those hoping to be.

One of the most rewarding parts of our jobs in restaurant management is the ability to help people grow professionally and personally. Kelly and I both have worked with some really amazing people, including entry level employees, managers, district managers, franchise owners, corporate support staff, corporate CEO's and even founders. We have learned from the best and now strive to give back to our team every day.

We work with a very diverse group of employees: people of various ages, different backgrounds, varying levels of work experience, educational differences, etc. All these people have different needs, expectations and personal goals. As managers we take responsibility for them and that is an enjoyable, creative, rewarding part of what we do. Take for example the entry level employee that is accepting his/her first job. We and the experience we provide, will impact them for the rest of their life. With more than 25% of all adults getting their start in a restaurant, we impact a lot of people. We have an obligation to society, in setting standards for work ethic, reliability and performance. We teach life lessons. Many of these entry level employees will go on to higher education or other careers. Some will become managers with us. One thing is for certain, they will always remember their first work experience.

We employ people in transition. They spend most of their career transitioning from one job to another, never staying in one place very long. They always have reasons for the excessive job hopping. Sometimes the person just hasn't found their niche, they have experienced a life changing event like death or divorce, or they had a bad job experience somewhere else. We have developed some very talented, loyal managers from this group. Again, it is so rewarding to help people grow and reach their potential in this business. I would like to add here, that restaurants employee a lot of women. We have more female managers than male. Schedule flexibility and promotional opportunities are two big reasons for that.

One of the special things we do in our current company that often impacts people in transition is to require a High School Diploma or GED for anyone that enters management. Our aunt, Mary Lou, has made this a priority and even picks up the bill for GED preparation classes. Mary Lou is involved in community programs to help Oregon children be successful in school. Kelly and I have even tutored individuals in various academics in preparation for GED testing. We believe education is important, whether the person stays with us, or life takes them elsewhere. When you care about the things that help people care about themselves, they care about the business. Re-read that sentence and think about it carefully. What's wrong with a win-win for everyone?

One of the employees that we helped several years ago, by encouraging the GED and promoting into management, recently returned home for a holiday. I didn't immediately recognize her, since it had been almost eight years later. However, the smile on her face took me back in time quickly. She came over to where I was sitting in the dining room, and went on to tell me that she was hoping to run into someone from the "old days". She began to cry when she introduced me to her young son. She told me that she remembered being so scared to take her GED test, and that she really didn't understand at the time why we insisted on it for a management position in fast food. As she wiped the tears from her eyes, and I tried to hold back mine, she went on to tell me about the job that she was currently in, and how well it paid. Without us, she felt like she would have never gotten the job because it too required an education. She said that none of it would have been possible without our help and encouragement. That day will forever be in my memory.

When young people get thrown from the tracks of life we believe they deserve a second chance. In our careers we come across employees that have been abandoned by their parents, or don't have anyone guiding them in life. Sometimes people need help and being able to help people is an important part of restaurant management.

We also employ people that have worked in the restaurant industry for years. This too is a great group of individuals. It is so personally rewarding to mentor, train, develop, and promote. We have wonderful people that aren't even aware of the talent and skills they possess. As a manager, we challenge people and guide them to reach their potential. These individuals are appreciative, motivated and loyal.

I enjoy bringing in new talented employees that intend to only work for a short time or part-time for extra money. Some of these individuals bring experiences from other industries and add so much value to our team. We have some skilled managers that decided to join us full time from this group.

In an unstable economy, many people are without work or are being forced to consider a career change. Would the restaurant industry be right for you? I don't know. But I hope you don't discount all the opportunities available, just because of false stereotypes. If you are an energetic, quick thinking, flexible, professional, with strong communication skills, this could be a viable career choice for you. We are really the same as any other business. We employ great people, strive to do the job right (QSC), manage the process, and make a profit (&P).

From Her:

I do enjoy getting the last word in. I like to compare the restaurant industry to where we live in Oregon. Most people don't know what a wonderful place this is to live, so it's not over crowded. Likewise, most people don't know how rewarding and gainful restaurants are, so opportunity is abundant.

Conclusion

In conclusion, we believe QSC, training and development, communication, follow-up, goals, planning and organization, not wasting, human resources, happy people and service can bring you success, as it has us. We hope our short book, in its simplicity, met your expectations. We hope to have helped or encouraged you in some small way. Maybe you now see the restaurant business through different eyes. We are what burger flippers look like. We truly love what we do and we wish the same success for you.

A final disclaimer:

We have shared experiences and made suggestions. We do not however, suggest being married and working together. As professionals, we possess qualities that complement one another. Find a complement you're not married to. Most couples could not work together the way we do. Who knows, our next book might be, *Flip-N-Out Married and Working Together.*

The Successful Manager

We believe a successful manager is created, much like a fine hamburger is. You begin with a strong quality base from which to build upon, QSC. Quality, service and cleanliness are what we focus on every day. Training and development are the meat of what we do. They must be done thoroughly. Like cheese, communication is critical. Without follow-up nothing gets done. Like a burger without mushrooms, why bother? Bacon comes next. It is expensive so don't waste it. Don't waste anything in fact. Then add a few pickles like happy employees. We need smiling faces to get the job done. Let's not forget the onion, or human resources. They are strong and hot- we need them for balance. Now spread the goals, planning and organization. They all work together, much like ketchup, mustard and mayonnaise. And finally, top it all off with a rewarding career!

Special Thanks

We thank all the talented employees and managers that we work with. You inspire us every day. Thank you to our many mentors along the way. Thank you to our Aunt (Mary Lou) and Uncle (Walt) who have been so supportive and have taught us much. Mary Lou is like a sister and put a lot of time into this project. We also appreciate our creative friend Toki Cavener, who photographed our cover. Thank you to Patti Baratta, who edited our book. And finally, we thank our families who always encourage us.

Contacts

To order additional copies of Flip-N-Burgers or for bulk
purchases, please visit us at:

www.Flip-N-Burgers.com

To contact Patti Baratta for editing:

pbaratta@centurytel.net

To contact Toki Cavener for photography:

www.tokisphotos.com

Made in the USA
San Bernardino, CA
02 April 2018